FORGED IN THE FIGHT

A 21 DAY BATTLE PLAN TO MANHOOD THROUGH THE LIFE OF JOSHUA

PASTOR JOSE VASQUEZ

Dedication

To the men who are tired of drifting and ready to rise, may you discover that the fight is not against you, it is forging you. You can become the kind of man who stays faithful, stands strong, and finishes well.

And to my wife, Annette, thank you for standing with me through the battles that shaped me, believing in what God was forming when the process was heavy, and loving me with strength, grace, and unwavering loyalty. This book carries your fingerprints more than you know.

Foreword

"Great faith," said Smith Wigglesworth,
"is the product of great fights."

All of us are fighting battles all the time—internal and external, emotional and spiritual. This should not dishearten us. Why? Such is life! No one gets a free pass when it comes to trials or temptations. But we must not forget this fact: we have a High Priest who not only empathizes with our weaknesses. He's also advocating on our behalf at the right hand of the Father. Jesus defeated sin at Calvary's cross, then He defeated death on the third day. Translation: the devil is a defeated foe. It's the victory Jesus won that makes us more than conquerors in Christ.

I have a rule of life: everyone is fighting a battle I know nothing about. Some battles are external, but most are internal. The flesh and the Spirit wage war against each other. The good news? We fight from a place of victory! Of course, that doesn't mean it doesn't take blood, sweat, and tears! If you're intent on fighting the good fight, this book is for you. I have much love and respect for my friend, Jose Vasquez. His leadership is battle-tested. His courage is contagious. And the wisdom that comes from obedience is imprinted on every page of this book.

If you've lost a few battles, you need to know that God's grace is sufficient. The God of second chances picks us up, dusts us off, and gives us another go. And if you learn the lessons God is trying to teach you through the tough times, it's not for naught. Nine times out of ten, success is well-managed failure. And that's where this book enters the equation. It will give you the courage to keep fighting the good fight and provide you with tactics and techniques to win in spiritual warfare. Regardless of the *battle you're fighting, it's time to "strengthen your feeble arms and weak knees."*

**- Mark Batterson,
NYT Bestselling Author of *The Circle Maker***

Table of Contents

Introduction

Today, we begin the journey—a journey where men stop sitting on the sidelines and step into the fight that shapes them. A journey where excuses quiet down, clarity rises, and the man God intended you to be begins to come forward; this is where the forging begins.

Every man feels the tension between who he is and who he knows he could be. You feel it in the moments when sleep will not come because something in you is unsettled. You feel it when responsibility calls louder than your confidence. You feel it when something deep inside whispers that there is more in you than what you have been living out. That tension is not a flaw. It is a signal. It is God inviting you into the fight that grows boys into warriors and wanderers into men.

The life of Joshua is not the story of a man who showed up ready. It is the story of a man's formation. He was shaped in quiet places where nobody clapped for him. He was strengthened through battles he did not choose. He was prepared through moments that did not feel spiritual or glamorous. Before Joshua ever stepped into the Promised Land, he had to step into the fight happening inside him. He had to confront fear, uncertainty, responsibility, and the weight of what God was calling him to carry. It was in those moments that God forged the man he would become.

This devotional is your twenty-one-day battle plan. Not to make you perfect but to make you prepared. Not to make you impressive but to ground you. Not to push you to perform, but to help you grow stronger from the inside out.

For the next twenty-one days, you will walk with Joshua, but more importantly, God will walk with you. You will see how God builds courage, confronts fear, trains obedience, and calls men to a deeper level than they imagined. You will see that God is not looking for men who can act religiously. Instead, He is shaping men who can stand when life gets heavy, men who can walk through pressure, temptation, responsibility, and calling without losing who they are.

Maybe you have been drifting for a long time; maybe you have been leading from your pain instead of your purpose; maybe you have been hiding behind busyness, success, or silence; maybe you are tired of surviving and ready to fight for the life God created you for. Wherever you find yourself on this first day, you are not stepping into this alone. God begins the forging with whatever you bring Him today.

Each day will bring a truth that stretches you and calls something out of you. You will face the fight within before you ever face the battles around you. Joshua learned that victory always begins before a sword is ever lifted. It starts in the mind, in the heart, and in the will of a man who decides he will no longer live small. This journey is not a study. It is not about collecting information. It is about formation. About becoming. The goal is not inspiration. The goal is <u>rising</u>.

By the time you reach day twenty-one, you will not be the same man who started. You will think differently. You will see differently. You will carry yourself differently. You will make decisions from a position of strength rather than fear. You will step into your relationships, your work, and your calling with greater clarity and courage.

Forging is not easy, but it is worth it, because the man you are becoming is worth it. So take a breath. Plant your feet. Lift your head. The fight is not against you; it is *for* you. Today, you step into the ring—the forging begins <u>now</u>.

DAY 1:
When God Calls Your Name

When God calls your name, He is not reminding you of what you have lost. He is revealing who you are becoming.

"After the death of Moses the servant of the Lord, the Lord said to Joshua son of Nun, Moses' aide: "Moses my servant is dead. Now then, you and all these people, get ready to cross the Jordan River into the land I am about to give to them, to the Israelites."
— Joshua 1:1–2, NIV

Inside the Fight

There comes a day in every man's life when the weight shifts to his shoulders. You can feel it even when no one else sees it yet—something in the air changes. A season ends, a leader steps aside, a father figure is gone, a safety net breaks, and suddenly, you are no longer standing behind someone. You are standing where they once stood.

Take Joshua, for example. He found himself here when Moses was gone. The man he leaned on, learned from, and looked to was no longer in front of him. Then God broke the silence, not to a crowd, not to a committee, not to a team. He spoke to Joshua. One man. One name. One moment.

Here is what I want you to see. God did not simply announce the end of a chapter. He put the weight of what was next on Joshua's shoulders. And God did not place that kind of weight on a man He had not already prepared. While Joshua served in the background, God quietly shaped him, forming character and forging strength long before Joshua ever felt ready.

Similarly, this is where many men freeze. We feel the pressure but not the preparation. We feel the responsibility but doubt our readiness. We start asking whether we are enough or have what it takes, but lean in for this. God does not call you based on how comfortable you feel. He calls you based on who He designed you to be.

Joshua's calling is not about filling Moses' shoes. It is about stepping into Joshua's strength. It is about becoming the man God always saw in him. The same is true for you. God is not asking you to become someone else. He is calling out the man He already built within you.

You are standing here because something in your life has shifted. Something ended. Something changed.

And in the middle of that shift, God is calling your name. Not to expose you, but to help you evolve. Not to embarrass you, but to build you. This shift is not the end of who you were; it is the beginning of who you are becoming.

Today's Battle Plan

"But now, this is what the Lord says, he who created you, Jacob, he who formed you, Israel. "Do not fear, for I have redeemed you, I have summoned you by name, you are mine." — Isaiah 43:1, NIV

God is not guessing about you. He created you with intention, redeemed you with purpose, and calls you by name because you belong to Him.

Take the Next Step

Choose one place in your life where you have been waiting for someone else to take the lead. Make one clear decision and take one concrete action that moves you from staying in the background to stepping into the responsibility God has already placed on your name.

The Truth You Need to Face

1. What have you been leaning on that is no longer available to you?

    ____

    ____

    ____

2. When life forced you into responsibility before you felt ready, what did you learn about yourself in that moment?

    ____

    ____

    ____

3. What would begin to shift in you today if you stopped grieving what ended and started preparing for what God is developing in you now?

    ____

    ____

    ____

DAY 2:
The Strength to Stand

Strength is not about how much you can carry. It is about who holds you.

"No one will be able to stand against you all the days of your life. As I was with Moses, so I will be with you. I will never leave you nor forsake you."
— Joshua 1:5, NIV

Inside the Fight

Before God ever gave Joshua a battle plan, He gave him a promise. Joshua was stepping into a role that would test him deeply. He would stand in front of people who remembered Moses, face enemies who wanted him dead, and feel the pull of fears he had never encountered before. God knew all of that long before Joshua did. So God anchored him in the one thing that would steady him—his presence.

Most men try to stand on their own. We grit our teeth, push through, and pretend we are not shaken. We carry pressure we never talk about and act as if we have it under control. Somewhere along the way, we start believing that strength means holding everything together on our own. No wonder we feel tired on the inside while trying to look tough on the outside.

Lean in here. Real strength does not begin with your performance. It starts with God's presence. When God says, "I will be with you, I will never leave you nor forsake you," He is not offering Joshua a comforting thought. He is giving him a foundation to stand on. A man is only as steady as what he stands on. If you stand on your own ability, you will shake. If you stand on God's presence, you may feel the pressure, but you will never be alone under it.

Joshua would face critics, enemies, battles, and moments that shook him. God never promised those things would not come. He promised that Joshua would never face them alone.

The same is true for you. You are not expected to carry the weight of your life by yourself. You are not meant to be the husband, father, leader, or man you want to be in your own strength. God is not watching from a distance. He stands with you in the middle of it, even when you do not feel Him. The question is never whether God is present. The question is whether you will choose to stand like He is.

Today's Battle Plan

"So we say with confidence, 'the Lord is my helper, I will not be afraid, what can mere mortals do to me?'" — Hebrews 13:6, NIV

You do not have to be the strongest man in the room when the Lord is your helper. Confidence grows when you trust more in the God who stands with you than in the strength you think you need to have.

Take the Next Step

Identify one place in your life where fear or pressure has been causing you to pull back. Talk honestly with God about it, then take a straightforward action that reflects confidence in His presence with you rather than in your own ability to manage it.

The Truth You Need to Face

1. What pressure in your life are you trying to manage on your own?

____

____

____

2. Where do you struggle most to believe that God is
   truly with you?

   ____

   ____

   ____

3. If you lived today as if God were standing right
   beside you, how would that change the way you
   show up?

   ____

   ____

   ____

DAY 3:
The Courage to Obey

Courage is not the absence of fear; it is the decision to obey even when fear is present.

"Be strong and courageous, because you will lead these people to inherit the land I swore to their ancestors to give them." — Joshua 1:6, NIV

Inside the Fight

Here is where the journey gets real. God does not tell Joshua to be courageous so he can feel brave; He tells him to be fearless because obedience will require it. Joshua is not just stepping into a new assignment. He is stepping into a land filled with giants, fortified cities, and battles waiting on the other side of his obedience. And God knows something Joshua is still learning. A man cannot walk out of God's purpose without walking through moments that demand courage.

Obedience has a way of stretching you. It pulls you out of convenience and pushes you into confrontation, not with people, but with the fear you have carried, the

21

doubt you have hidden, and the mindset you have lived with for too long. Obedience is costly. It will confront the version of you that prefers control and comfort.

Here's what I want you to see. Courage in Scripture is rarely loud. It is often quiet, steady, and persistent. It looks like taking the next step when your legs feel heavy. It looks like moving forward when your mind is still trying to talk you out of it. It looks like trusting God more than you trust your fear.

God had already promised the land to Joshua. The future was secure, but that promise would remain intact only if Joshua obeyed. Promise does not replace obedience; it empowers it. God gives the land, but the man must take the step.

You may not be facing giants, but you know what it feels like to stand in front of something bigger than your confidence. Maybe it is a decision you keep avoiding. It could be a habit you need to break or a conversation you know you need to have. Maybe it is stepping into a role that feels too heavy for you. Courage is not feeling ready. Courage is obeying anyway.

There are places God wants to take you that cannot be reached through comfort. Those places require courage. The steady kind. The quiet kind. The type that obeys even while your heart is still sorting through the weight of what God is asking.

Today's Battle Plan

"For God has not given us a spirit of fear,
but of power, love, and a sound mind."
— 2 Timothy 1:7, NIV

Fear does not come from God, and neither does the hesitation that tries to hold you back. God has already placed courage within you, even if it feels small. Use what He has given you.

Take the Next Step

Choose one thing you know God has been asking of you, something fear has been standing in front of. Do one concrete act of obedience today, even if it feels small, and trust that courage grows with every step you take.

The Truth You Need to Face

1. What has God asked of you that fear has been talking you out of?

____

____

____

2. Where is courage missing from your decisions right
    now?

____

24

____

____

3. What will it cost you if you stay where you are and
    never step into the obedience God is calling you
    toward?

____

____

____

DAY 4:
The Fight for Focus

You cannot move forward if you keep
looking sideways.

"Be strong and very courageous.
Be careful to obey all the laws my servant Moses
gave you, do not turn from it to the right or to the
left, that you may be successful wherever you go."
— Joshua 1:7, NIV

Inside the Fight

When God speaks to Joshua here, notice the shift. God is not just calling him to strength or courage anymore. He is calling him to focus. "Be careful," He says, because God knows that sometimes the fiercest battles a man faces are not against the enemy in front of him, they are against the distractions around him.

Here's where it gets real. Most men do not lose ground because they stop believing. They lose ground because they stop focusing. A little compromise. A small detour. One excuse that feels harmless. One delay that feels justified. And before long, the edge dulls, and the heart drifts. You are still moving, but not in the direction God intended.

God is telling Joshua something every man needs to hear. You do not get to where I am taking you by being casual. You get there by staying centered. You get there by keeping My Word front and center, especially when life pulls at you from every side.

The world will always offer shortcuts. Ego will always whisper that you don't need the discipline. Pressure will tempt you to look for the easier road. And if your focus slips, even a little, your steps will follow.

Lean in here. If you want to walk in your calling, you have to be a man of focus. Not just focused when you feel inspired, but also when things are calm. You must focus every day, and focus when it is inconvenient. Focus when your emotions pull you in another direction. Focus when your old habits try to drag you back.

Joshua was stepping into a future that required clarity. You are, too. A man becomes who God calls him to be when he refuses to keep looking sideways and chooses instead to stay locked in on what God says.

Today's Battle Plan

*"Let your eyes look straight ahead, fix your gaze
directly before you. Give careful thought to the paths
for your feet and be steadfast in all your ways."*
— Proverbs 4:25–26, NIV

Focus is not an accident. It is a choice you make every day, a choice to lift your eyes from what distracts you and fix them on where God is leading you.

Take the Next Step

Do a distraction audit. Identify one thing that has been stealing too much of your attention, and set it aside for the next three days. Replace that space with time in the Word, even if it is just a few minutes each day. Let God reset your focus.

The Truth You Need to Face

1. What has been pulling your focus away from God lately?

---

2. How have minor distractions been shaping your decisions as a man?

____

____

____

3. What would shift in your life if you were fully dialed in to what God is saying?

____

____

____

DAY 5:
Winning the War Within

The battle in your head shapes the future
in your hands.
*"Keep this Book of the Law always on your lips,
meditate on it day and night, so that you may be
careful to do everything written in it.
Then you will be prosperous and successful."*
— Joshua 1:8, NIV

Inside the Fight

There is a battle you can see, and there is a battle you cannot. The visible battles get your attention, but the invisible one often decides everything. God tells Joshua to meditate on His Word day and night, not as a religious routine, but as a survival strategy. God knows something every man eventually realizes. The war is won or lost long before you swing a sword. It is won or lost in the mind.

The most destructive attacks rarely come from the outside. They rise quietly within you. They sound like old fears and familiar insecurities. They whisper, "You

29

are not enough. You will always fall back. You cannot change." These lies are subtle but powerful when left unchecked. They blur your focus, weaken your courage, and slowly pull you away from who God is calling you to be.

Lean in for this. Those voices do not get the final word unless you let them. God gives Joshua a different strategy. Replace lies with truth. Let His Word fill the space where doubt used to live. Let it shift how you think, how you see yourself, how you see God, how you see the fight in front of you.

The Word is your weapon. Not willpower, because willpower will eventually run out. Not distractions, because distractions only delay the battle. God's Word is what renews your mind, strengthens your resolve, and breaks the cycles you keep trying to fix on your own. Speak it. Sit with it. Carry it in your thoughts throughout the day. Let it lead you before your emotions do.

Here is what you need to remember. When your mind shifts, your choices shift. When your choices shift, your direction shifts. When your direction shifts, your life begins to move toward the man you were created to be. The war within is not something to fear. It is something to win.

Today's Battle Plan

"Do not conform to the pattern of this world, but be transformed by the renewing of your mind."
— Romans 12:2, NIV

Transformation begins where your thoughts begin. God renews your mind so you can step into the life He has designed for you, not the one your past has conditioned you to expect.

Take the Next Step

Choose one lie you have been believing about yourself, one thought that keeps circling back and weakening you. Confront it with Scripture today. Speak the truth out loud and let it interrupt the pattern that has been shaping you from the inside out.

The Truth You Need to Face

1. What lies have you been believing about yourself lately?

____

____

____

2. How consistently are you filling your mind with what God says?

____

____

____

3. What would shift in your decisions if your mind were anchored in Scripture instead of insecurity?

____

____

____

DAY 6:
The Other Side of Fear

Fear screams loudest at the edge of breakthrough.
*"I know that the Lord has given you this land
and that a great fear of you has fallen on us,
so that all who live in this country are melting
in fear because of you."*
— Joshua 2:9, NIV

Inside the Fight

Joshua sends two spies into the land, expecting a report about giants, walls, and danger. What they hear instead from Rahab changes everything. While Israel has been afraid of what lies ahead, the enemy has been fearful of them. Let that sink in for a moment. The very thing they feared was already trembling.

Fear has a way of lying to you. It distorts what is real. It takes your eyes off what God said and fixes them on everything that might go wrong. It makes shadows look bigger than they are. It convinces you that the obstacle in front of you is stronger than the God within you.

Lean in here. What if the fear you feel is nothing more than intimidation from something already defeated? What if the enemy's loudest tactic is simply hoping you never discover that he is the one who is afraid? Joshua's men walk into Jericho expecting resistance, but they find a city melting in fear because God had already gone before them.

Many men get stuck here. Not because the challenge is too great, but because the fear feels too loud. Fear tells you to stay in the wilderness. To settle. To stand still. To talk yourself out of the very thing your spirit knows God is leading you toward. But the land was already theirs. The promise was already spoken. The outcome was already leaning in their favor.

Notice something important here. The enemy was terrified of Israel before Israel ever knew it. The very thing you have been afraid to face may already be losing its grip. God has been working ahead of you, preparing ground you have not even stepped on yet. Do not let your mind talk you out of what God has already placed in your hand.

Today's Battle Plan

*"For the Spirit God gave us does not make us timid,
but gives us power, love, and self-discipline."*
— 2 Timothy 1:7, NIV

Fear does not come from God. Courage does. And the Spirit within you is stronger than the fear that has been standing in front of you.

Take the Next Step

Write down the one fear that keeps circling your mind, the one that has been paralyzing your next step. Then write beside it, "My God is greater." Say it out loud. Walk through your day as if that fear is already losing its power, because it is.

The Truth You Need to Face

1. What fear has been holding you back from stepping into what God has spoken over your life?

____

____

____

2. How does Joshua 2:9 shift the way you see whatever
   stands in front of you?

   ____

   ____

   ____

3. What would change in your decisions if you believed
   the battle is already tipping in your favor?

   ____

   ____

   ____

DAY 7:
When Waiting Isn't Wasted

If God is not leading, you are not moving;
you are wandering.

*"When you see the ark of the covenant of the Lord
your God, and the Levitical priests carrying it,
you are to move out from your positions and follow
it… Then you will know which way to go,
since you have never been this way before."*
— Joshua 3:3–4, NIV

Inside the Fight

Joshua gives the people complex yet straightforward instructions. Wait until you see the ark move. The ark represents the presence of God. In other words, do not move until He does. For men who have been wandering for years, this instruction is both grounding and uncomfortable. Waiting requires trust, and trust exposes what is really driving you.

Most men struggle with waiting. We would rather act, fix, decide, or force momentum than sit still and listen. Waiting feels weak to us. It feels unproductive.

But here is the truth most men miss. Movement without God is not progress. It is disobedience dressed up as confidence.

There is a difference between passivity and patience. Passivity avoids responsibility. Patience embraces restraint. Passivity checks out. Patience stays alert. One drifts. The other stands ready. Joshua is not telling the people to do nothing. He is teaching them how to watch, follow, and move at the right time.

Lean in for this. What you often call delay, God may be calling development. While you are waiting, God is sharpening your discernment. He is training your eyes to follow instead of lead. He is teaching you to hear Him before you react. You have never been this way before, and that is exactly why you cannot rely on instinct alone. You need God in front of you.

Waiting is not wasted when it keeps you aligned with God's presence. It is wasted only when you rush ahead and lose sight of Him. The man you are becoming is not revealed only by how boldly you move, but by how faithfully you wait when God says stay.

Today's Battle Plan

*"Trust in the Lord with all your heart and lean not on
your own understanding. In all your ways submit to
him, and he will make your paths straight."*
— Proverbs 3:5–6, NIV

Trust is choosing God's direction over your impulse.
When you submit your timing to Him, He takes responsibility for the path ahead.

Take the Next Step

Before making any significant decision today, pause
and pray honestly. Ask, "God, are You leading this, or
am I trying to force it?" Sit with the question long
enough to listen, then respond with obedience rather
than urgency.

The Truth You Need to Face

1. Where are you most tempted to rush ahead of God
   right now?

____

____

____

2. What has impatience cost you in past decisions?

____

____

____

3. What would it look like to trust God enough to wait
    for His direction instead of pushing for your own
    timing?

____

____

____

DAY 8:
Step into the Unknown

The water does not part until
your foot moves forward.
*"Now the Jordan is at flood stage all during harvest.
Yet as soon as the priests who carried the ark
reached the Jordan and their feet touched the
water's edge, the water from upstream
stopped flowing."*
— Joshua 3:15–16, NIV

Inside the Fight

The timing could not have been worse. The Jordan was overflowing its banks. The water was high, fast, and dangerous. If God was going to move, this was not how most of us would have planned it. Yet this is exactly where God tells the priests to step. Not after the waters recede. Not when it feels safer. Right into the flood.

Notice how God works here. He does not part the water first. He waits for movement. The miracle does not come before obedience. It follows it. The priests must put their feet in the water before anything changes. Obedience is not recklessness; obedience is trust.

Here is where faith gets uncomfortable. We like clarity before commitment. We want guarantees before we move. We pray for God to make a way, while God waits for us to take a step. But faith does not wait for ideal conditions. Faith responds to God even when the conditions look impossible.

Here is what you need to see. God often calls men into places they have never been so He can show them who they have never been. If the water parts first, you never learn to trust Him. If the ground stays dry, you never grow. The unknown is not punishment. It is an invitation.

Stepping into the unknown does not mean ignoring wisdom. It means responding to God when He speaks, even if your emotions lag behind your obedience. When God says go, what stands in your way does not get the final word. The moment your obedience hits the water, God makes a way.

Today's Battle Plan

*"Now faith is confidence in what we hope for
and assurance about what we do not see."*
— Hebrews 11:1, NIV

Faith is not pretending you are fearless. It is moving forward while you trust God with what you cannot yet see.

Take the Next Step

Identify one place where you have been waiting for everything to make sense before you move. Take one small, intentional step today in the direction God has been prompting you. Do not wait for the conditions to change. Step forward and trust God to meet you there.

The Truth You Need to Face

1. Where have you been waiting for clarity instead of acting on faith?

____

____

____

2. What are you afraid might happen if you step forward before you feel ready?

____

____

____

3. How has hesitation delayed progress in your life before, and what might change if you moved now?

____

____

____

DAY 9:
Set a Marker

If you do not mark what God has done, you will begin to doubt what He is doing.
*"In the future, when your children ask you,
'What do these stones mean?'
tell them…'the Lord your God did this.'"*
— Joshua 4:6–7, NIV

Inside the Fight

After the river is crossed and the danger is behind them, God does something unexpected. He does not tell Joshua to press forward. He tells him to go back. Go back into the river. Pick up stones. Set a marker.

Here is why that matters. Men forget. Not because we are careless, but because life keeps moving. One challenge gives way to the next. One victory fades as the next battle rises. And if we do not pause to remember, we slowly lose sight of how often God has carried us.

These stones were not decoration. They were testimony. They were physical reminders that God made a way where there was no way and stopped the waters, that He kept His promise. God knew there would be days ahead when fear would resurface and confidence would waver. On those days, the stones would speak.

Every man needs markers. Moments you can point back to when doubt starts talking. Seasons where God showed up in a way you could not explain. Times when you stepped forward unsure, and God held you steady. When the fight gets fierce later, you will need something to say, "I have seen Him move before. He will do it again."

And this is not just for you. Your family needs it. Your brothers need it. Your future needs it. When you mark what God has done, you create an anchor for the days when the waters start rising again.

Today's Battle Plan

"Praise be to the Lord, to God our Savior,
who daily bears our burdens."
— Psalm 68:19, NIV

God has been carrying you longer than you realize. Remembering His faithfulness strengthens your trust for what lies ahead.

Take the Next Step

Take time today to write down one moment where God clearly came through for you. Place it somewhere visible this week. Let it remind you that the same God who moved then is still moving now.

The Truth You Need to Face

1. What moment of God's faithfulness have you rushed past without reflecting on it?

____

____

____

2. Why is it easier to forget what God has done when
   new battles appear?

   ____

   ____

   ____

3. What marker could you establish today that would
   strengthen your faith tomorrow?

   ____

   ____

   ____

DAY 10:
Reclaim What's Been Cut Off

You cannot conquer what you are still covering.
"At that time the Lord said to Joshua, 'Make flint knives and circumcise the Israelites again.'"
— Joshua 5:2, NIV

Inside the Fight

This moment in the story feels abrupt, even uncomfortable, and that is intentional. Israel has crossed the Jordan. The promise is within reach. Momentum is building. And then God stops everything. Before the first battle is fought, before Jericho ever comes into view, God turns His attention inward.

Circumcision was not about ritual. It was about identity. It was the sign that marked these men as belonging to God. For forty years in the wilderness, that mark had been neglected. These men had survived, but they had not fully surrendered. Now, standing on the edge of promise, God addresses what had been left undone.

Here is where this meets your life. Before God increases your influence, He often deepens your surrender. Before He gives you new ground to take, He deals with what has been numbing you, hiding in you, or quietly shaping you beneath the surface. This process is not punishment. It is preparation.

Lean in here. God is not after your performance. He is after your heart. He is not trying to shame you. He is trying to restore you. Some of the things God asks you to release are private and painful. Old habits that helped you cope. Wounds you learned to live with—patterns you buried instead of confronting. Surgery always hurts, but it heals what pretending never will.

This moment also required vulnerability. These men were exposed. Unable to fight. Unable to defend themselves. They had to trust that obedience was safer than armor. That surrender was stronger than self-protection. Sometimes the bravest thing a man can do is let God touch the places he has been guarding.

If God is asking you to cut something away, it is not because He wants to take something from you. It is because that thing does not belong to who you are becoming. You cannot carry old wounds, hidden sin, or unchecked habits into new territory and expect wholeness. Healing does not happen by avoidance. It happens when you trust God enough to let Him work where it hurts.

Today's Battle Plan

"Search me, God, and know my heart,
test me and know my anxious thoughts.
See if there is any offensive way in me,
and lead me in the way everlasting."
— Psalm 139:23–24, NIV

David's prayer is not soft; it is a surrender prayer. David is inviting God into the places most men avoid: motives, fears, triggers, and hidden compromises. He is saying, Lord, I do not want to manage my image; I want You to heal my heart. This is how you reclaim what has been cut off. You stop negotiating with what is quietly killing you and start agreeing with what God is clearly revealing. You cannot conquer what you are still covering, so bring it into the light and let God lead you out—not just out of sin, but into the way everlasting.

Take the Next Step

Get alone with God today for ten minutes, no phone, no noise. Read Psalm 139:23–24 out loud. Then write down one pattern you have been covering, excusing, or hiding, and one step of obedience God is prompting you to take this week. After you write it, choose one trusted brother and tell him the one thing you know has to change, then ask him to check in with you twice this week.

The Truth You Need to Face

1. What am I protecting from God because I am afraid of what He will ask me to cut away?

    ____

    ____

    ____

2. What have I normalized in my life that is quietly numbing my conviction and weakening my strength?

    ____

    ____

    ____

3. If God gave me a new territory today, what part of my inner life would sabotage it if it stayed untouched?

    ____

    ____

    ____

DAY 11:
When God's Way Makes No Sense

Victory does not require understanding;
it requires obedience.

*"Now the gates of Jericho were securely barred
because of the Israelites. No one went out and no
one came in. Then the Lord said to Joshua,
'See, I have delivered Jericho into your hands,
along with its king and its fighting men.'"*
— Joshua 6:1–2, NIV

Inside the Fight

Jericho is locked down. The walls are high. The enemy is fortified and ready. Here is the moment every man expects a strategy that makes sense. Weapons. Positioning. Strength. Force. Instead, God gives Joshua instructions that sound almost foolish. March. Be quiet. Walk. Wait. Trust.

This is where obedience collides with ego. God's plan does not appeal to Joshua's instincts or experience. It does not feed his need to feel powerful. It forces him to trust God more than his own understanding. And that is often where the real fight begins.

Here is what you need to notice. God tells Joshua the victory is already his before a single step is taken. Jericho is delivered, even though the walls are still standing. The promise comes before the proof. But the proof will only come if Joshua obeys a plan that feels uncomfortable and unconventional.

Many men struggle here. We want God's promises, but we also want control. We seek clarity but resist humility. We want victory, but only if it comes through methods that protect our pride. Jericho exposes that tension. God's way strips Joshua of the illusion that strength comes from force. It reminds him that obedience is the real weapon.

Lean in for this. Sometimes God's instructions feel quiet when you want noise. Slow when you want speed. Simple when you want impressive. But God is not trying to make you look strong. He is teaching you how to trust Him fully. The walls of Jericho did not fall because the people shouted well. They fell because the people obeyed well.

You may be facing a situation that feels locked up and immovable. You may be waiting for God to tell you how to fight, while God is asking if you will follow. Victory does not always come through what feels powerful. Sometimes it comes through obedience that looks foolish to everyone else.

Today's Battle Plan

"For though we live in the world, we do not wage war as the world does. The weapons we fight with are not the weapons of the world. On the contrary, they have divine power to demolish strongholds."
— 2 Corinthians 10:3–4, NIV

God's power is not limited to human methods. When you trust His way, even when it makes no sense, He does what you cannot do on your own.

Take the Next Step

Identify one area where you have been resisting God's instruction because it does not align with your instincts or pride. Choose obedience today, even if it feels simple, slow, or unseen, and trust God with the outcome.

The Truth You Need to Face

1. Where are you tempted to rely on your own strength instead of God's direction?

____

____

____

2. What instruction from God have you been dismissing because it does not make sense to you?

____

____

____

3. How might obedience open the door to a breakthrough you cannot force on your own?

____

____

____

DAY 12:
The Power of Staying the Course

Breakthrough often comes after a period of
obedience that feels repetitive and unrewarding.
*"March around the city once with all the armed men.
Do this for six days. Have seven priests carry
trumpets of rams' horns in front of the ark. On the
seventh day, march around the city seven times,
with the priests blowing the trumpets."*
— Joshua 6:3–4, NIV

Inside the Fight

God's instructions for Jericho were not just strange; they were repetitive. Walk. Circle. Go home. Then do it again tomorrow. And the next day. And the next. No visible progress. No cracks in the wall. No signs that anything was changing. This inactivity is where many men quit.

We are wired for results. We want feedback. We want evidence that what we are doing is working. When obedience feels repetitive and unrewarding, doubt starts to creep in. We begin to wonder whether we heard God correctly; we question whether the effort is worthwhile and whether we are wasting our time.

However, here is what Joshua had to learn, and what you need to know, too. God was not just tearing down walls. He was building men—every lap around Jericho trained discipline. Every silent step strengthened trust. Every day, they showed up without results and forged obedience that did not depend on outcomes.

Lean in here. Consistency is not glamorous, but it is powerful. Most breakthroughs are not won in moments of intensity. They are won in seasons of faithfulness. Men drift not because they fail once, but because they stop doing the simple things that keep them aligned with God.

Joshua and the people stayed the course even when nothing changed on the outside. And all the while, God was working in ways they could not see. The walls did not fall on the first day, but obedience put pressure on them at every step.

You may be praying, showing up, resisting temptation, or making better choices with no immediate reward. Do not mistake silence for absence. God often waits until obedience is complete before He releases the breakthrough.

Today's Battle Plan

*"Let us not become weary in doing good,
for at the proper time we will reap a harvest
if we do not give up."*
— Galatians 6:9, NIV

God honors faithfulness over flash. Staying the course keeps you positioned for what He is preparing to release.

Take the Next Step

Identify one area where you are tempted to quit because you are not seeing results. Commit to staying faithful for one more day. Show up again. Trust that consistent obedience is doing more than you can see.

The Truth You Need to Face

1. Where have you been tempted to give up because progress feels slow?

2. What simple obedience have you neglected because it no longer feels rewarding?

____

____

____

3. How might consistency be forging something in you that instant results never could?

____

____

____

DAY 13:
The Strength to Stay Silent

Sometimes the most decisive move a man can make is knowing when not to speak.

"Joshua had commanded the army, 'Do not give a war cry, do not raise your voices, do not say a word until the day I tell you to shout. Then shout.'"
— Joshua 6:10, NIV

Inside the Fight

This part of the Jericho story often gets overlooked. Before the shouting, before the collapse, before the victory, there was silence. God tells Joshua to command the men not to speak—no trash talk. No explaining. No reacting. Just obedience and restraint.

Let's be honest, absolute silence is not easy for men. Silence feels weak when your instincts want to defend, correct, or prove something. Silence feels risky when people are watching and questioning what you are doing. Silence can feel like losing ground when everything in you wants to respond. But God knew something Joshua was still learning. Uncontrolled words can undo disciplined obedience.

Here is where it gets real. Many men lose momentum not because they stop obeying God, but because they speak at the wrong time. Men often talk out of frustration. We vent out of fear. We explain when God never asked us to do so. And slowly, our words reveal impatience, insecurity, or pride that God is still trying to work out of us.

Lean in here. Silence is not passivity. It is discipline. It is under control. God was teaching these men how to follow without commentary. How to trust without explanation. How to stay aligned even when the plan looked strange, and the pressure to speak was real.

Joshua knew the shout would come. But timing mattered. Speaking too early would disrupt what God was doing, and the same applies to your life. There are moments when restraint protects the work God is forming in you. When silence keeps you focused, and holding your tongue keeps your heart steady.

Not every thought needs to be spoken. Not every feeling needs to be shared. Not every situation requires your opinion. Sometimes the most mature response is obedience without noise.

Today's Battle Plan

*"Those who guard their mouths and
their tongues keep themselves from calamity."*
— Proverbs 21:23, NIV

Wisdom often shows up as restraint. When you learn to control your words, you protect your peace and your progress.

Take the Next Step

Pay attention to your words today. Choose one situation where you would normally react, explain, or defend yourself, and intentionally stay silent. Ask God to show you when silence is strengthening you rather than costing you.

The Truth You Need to Face

1. Where do you tend to speak too quickly instead of staying disciplined?

____

____

____

2. How have your words created unnecessary conflict
    or distraction in the past?

    ____

    ____

    ____

3. What might God be protecting or building in you
    through silence right now?

    ____

    ____

    ____

DAY 14:
Guard the Ground You've Gained

The battle may be over, but victory is secured by what you protect after battles are won.

"But keep away from the devoted things, so that you will not bring about your own destruction by taking any of them. Otherwise, you will make the camp of Israel liable to destruction and bring trouble on it."
— Joshua 6:18, NIV

Inside the Fight

Joshua 6:18 is one of those verses that hits men right where we live. Jericho is about to fall. The breakthrough is right in front of them. Momentum is building. And right there, in the middle of all that victory talk, God draws a line and says, "Do not touch what I have set apart."

Here is what I want you to see. Most men assume the fight is over when the walls fall. But some of the most dangerous moments come after the win. When you have progress, you start to relax. When you have momentum, you start to assume you are safe. When you finally get a breakthrough, you begin to think you have earned the right to take whatever you want. That is when a man becomes vulnerable.

God calls the devoted things off limits for a reason. Not because He is trying to keep them from enjoying the victory, but because He is protecting the victory from becoming a trap. Some things look like rewards, but they are really bait. They promise satisfaction, but they poison the soul. They make you feel like you are taking something, when in reality, something is taking you.

This is where discipline matters. Boundaries are not punishment. They are protection. God knows that what you tolerate after a win can undo what you fought for to get there. A man can conquer out there and still be defeated in here if he does not guard his heart and his appetite.

Some of the most damaging decisions men make happen when the pressure is off. When the adrenaline fades. When nobody is watching as closely, when you tell yourself you deserve a little something. You deserve it after all you have been through. You've earned it after the fight. Mindsets like these are how men open the door to trouble.

Lean in for this: God is not just interested in giving you victories. He is building you into a man who can handle victory. A man who can win and still stay clean. A man who can advance without drifting. A man who can take ground without taking what does not belong.

The battle is not only about breaking walls. It is about guarding the ground. Because the win is not the finish line. The win is the responsibility to live differently now that God brought you through.

Today's Battle Plan

*"So, if you think you are standing firm,
be careful that you do not fall."*
— 1 Corinthians 10:12, NIV

Winning can make a man careless, but God is teaching you how to stay clean after the breakthrough. The boundary is not God withholding from you; it is God protecting what He just brought you into.

Take the Next Step

Identify one boundary you have been tempted to blur lately, something you have been calling small, but you know is pulling at you. Make one clear decision today to reinforce the boundary: remove the access point, send the text, delete the app, cancel the plan, and choose the version of you that can handle victory.

The Truth You Need to Face

1. What boundary have you been tempted to cross because you feel like you earned it after the fight?

____

____

____

2. Where do you tend to get most vulnerable after a win, when the pressure is off, and your guard is down?

____

____

____

3. What practical guardrail do you need to put in place today so your victory does not become tomorrow's regret?

____

____

____

DAY 15:
Clean House

God cannot bless what you are still hiding.

"But the Israelites were unfaithful in regard to the devoted things; Achan son of Karmi, the son of Zabdi, the son of Zerah, of the tribe of Judah, took some of them. So the Lord's anger burned against Israel."
— Joshua 7:1, NIV

Inside the Fight

Joshua 7 is a significant turning point in the story. Jericho falls, victory is fresh, momentum is real, and then Israel loses to a much smaller battle. The reason is not a lack of strength. It is a lack of integrity. One man hides what God said to leave alone, and the cost is higher than he imagined.

Here is what I want you to see. Hidden compromise is never private. Achan may have buried it under his tent, but it did not stay there. His secret eventually permeated the entire camp. Achan brought confusion where there should have been confidence, weakness where there should have been strength, and defeat where there should have been progress.

This is why Scripture keeps calling men into the light. Not because God is trying to embarrass you, but because what you hide has a way of shaping you. It will drain your peace. It will dull your discernment. It will make you tired in ways sleep cannot fix. Then you start wondering why you feel stuck, why your joy is thin, why your prayers feel distant, and why the next step feels heavier than it should.

Cleaning house is not about shame. It is about alignment. It is about agreeing with God that what is buried must be brought up so healing can happen, so that freedom can grow, and so that the next season is not sabotaged by yesterday's secret.

Lean in here: many men want public victory while protecting private compromise. We want God to bless what everyone can see while we keep a stash of what no one knows. But God loves you too much to let you build your life on divided ground. He is not only shaping what you do but also who you are. The man you are becoming cannot be built on hidden corners.

If something is in your tent, it is not just sitting there. It is costing you more than you know. God is inviting you to clean house, not so you can be condemned, but so you can be free.

*"Whoever conceals their sins does not prosper,
but the one who confesses and
renounces them finds mercy."*
— Proverbs 28:13, NIV

You are not protecting yourself by hiding; you are delaying your healing. Mercy is on the other side of confession, and God is not waiting to crush you; He is ready to restore you.

Take the Next Step

Do an integrity check today. Name the one compromise you have been keeping under the tent, then confess it honestly to God and renounce it, not in vague language, but specifically. If wisdom requires it, bring it into the light with one trusted brother who will pray with you and help you stay aligned.

The Truth You Need to Face

1. What is in your tent right now that you know God has been telling you to deal with?

____

____

____

2. How has compromise been affecting your peace, your relationships, or your confidence as a man?

____

____

____

3. What is one practical step you can take today to move from secrecy to freedom?

____

____

____

DAY 16:
Recover and Rise

Failure does not disqualify you; quitting does.
*"Then the Lord said to Joshua, 'Do not be afraid;
do not be discouraged. Take the whole army with
you, and go up and attack Ai.
For I have delivered it into your hands the king of Ai,
his people, his city and his land.'"*
— Joshua 8:1, NIV

Inside the Fight

Joshua knows what it feels like when momentum turns into embarrassment. After Jericho, Ai should have been easy. Instead, it became a public loss and a private weight. Men died. Confidence fell. The camp felt the sting of shame. Joshua tore his clothes and fell to the ground. Not because he was dramatic, but because he was carrying the ache of what had just happened and the fear of what it might mean.

Here is where many men get stuck. Not in failure itself, but in what failure whispers afterward. It tells you it is over. It tells you you are not built for this. It tells you that you blew your chance, and now your best move is to stay down, stay quiet, keep your head low, and live smaller than what God once put in your heart.

But notice what God does in Joshua 8. He does not cancel Joshua. He speaks to him. He steadies him. He calls him back to the mission. God does not ignore what happened; He addresses it, He corrects it, and then He restores momentum: Do not be afraid, do not be discouraged. Take the whole army with you. Go back. Fight again. God has already delivered the victory into your hands.

Lean in here: *this* is <u>grace</u>. Grace does not just forgive; it rebuilds. It does not just pardon; it re-commits. It does not just clean you up; it puts you back on your feet and sends you forward with clarity.

Manhood is not about avoiding every failure. It is about refusing to let failure have the final word. A strong man is not the man who never stumbles. A strong man is the man who is honest, learns, repents when needed, and then gets back up with wisdom and courage.

You may have taken a loss. You may have regret sitting on your chest. You may still hear the echo of what went wrong. But, hear this clearly: God is not done with you. You are still called. You are still chosen. And if you are breathing, you still have a mission.

Today's Battle Plan

"Though he may stumble, he will not fall,
for the Lord upholds him with his hand."
— Psalm 37:24, NIV

Your stumble does not scare God. His hand is still on you, and His grip is stronger than your failure. What held you then can hold you now.

Take the Next Step

Name the failure that has been holding you back. Then, say this out loud, "God's grace is bigger than this." Now, do one thing today that a defeated man would not do: reach out, apologize, take responsibility, restart the habit, reapply, re-engage, and take one practical step forward.

The Truth You Need to Face

1. What failure have you been letting define you more than God's grace?

____

____

____

2. Why does shame make it feel safer to stay down than to rise again?

____

____

____

3. What would change in your momentum if you got back up today and moved forward with humility and courage?

____

____

____

DAY 17:
Stay in the Fight

Victory belongs to the man who refuses to quit.
*"The Lord said to Joshua, 'Do not be afraid of them;
I have given them into your hand.
Not one of them will be able to withstand you.'"*
— Joshua 10:8, NIV

Inside the Fight

Some battles test your strength, and some battles test your staying power. Joshua 10 is one of those moments. Five kings come against Joshua at once. It is not a quick fight. It is not a clean fight. It is the kind of fight that keeps going longer than you expected; the kind that makes a man wonder if he is wearing out faster than the enemy is.

Here is where many men lose heart. Not because they do not believe in God, but because they expected it to be easier *by now*. They expected the temptation to be gone *by now*. They expected the marriage to feel better *by now*. They expected the doors to open by now. They expected the healing to be finished *by now*.

When the battle drags on, discouragement starts to whisper, "Maybe *you are losing.*"

But notice what God says to Joshua: Do not be afraid of them. I have given them into your hand. Not one of them will be able to withstand you. God does not start by telling Joshua what he has to do. He begins by telling him what is already true. The outcome was settled, even though the process remained complex.

Lean in here. Just because your situation may still be hard does not mean you are losing. Resistance is not always a sign that you are off course. Sometimes resistance is confirmation that you are pressing into the proper ground. The enemy fights hardest when you are closest to taking territory. That is why staying in the fight matters.

Short sprints do not mark manhood. Instead, manhood is forged in long obedience. The kind of obedience that shows up again tomorrow. The kind that keeps praying when the answer feels delayed. The kind that keeps making the right choice when nobody sees it. The kind that keeps swinging when the battle is not over yet.

Here is where it gets real. The real question is not whether you will face resistance. *You will.* The question is whether you will remain faithful when it comes. Whether you will keep your hands on the plow. Whether you will keep your "yes" to God when the fight lasts longer than your patience wants.

You are closer than you think. Do not quit in the middle of what God is finishing. Do not let weariness talk you out of what obedience is building. Stay in the fight. Victory belongs to the man who refuses to quit.

Today's Battle Plan

*"Let us not become weary in doing good,
for at the proper time we will reap a harvest if
we do not give up."*
— Galatians 6:9, NIV

Weariness is real, but it should not lead you. God's timing is not your enemy, and faithfulness is never wasted.

Take the Next Step

Name the fight you have been backing away from: Your marriage, your purity, your calling, your discipline, and/or your healing. Say this out loud: "I will not quit." Then take one small step forward today. One phone call, one honest conversation, one prayer, one decision, one act of discipline, and allow that task to reposition you on solid ground.

The Truth You Need to Face

1. What area of your life have you been tempted to give up on lately?

2. Where have you misread resistance as failure instead of part of the process?

3. What would staying in the fight look like practically for you today, and what step can you take to prove it?

DAY 18:
Make the Sun Stand Still

If it doesn't stretch your faith, it might not be bold enough.

"On the day the Lord gave the Amorites over to Israel, Joshua said to the Lord in the presence of Israel: 'Sun, stand still over Gibeon, and you, moon, over the Valley of Aijalon.' So the sun stood still, and the moon stopped, till the nation avenged itself on its enemies, as it is written in the Book of Jashar. The sun stopped in the middle of the sky and delayed going down about a full day."
— Joshua 10:12–13, NIV

Inside the Fight

Here, we read one of the wildest moments in Joshua's story, and it isn't wild because Joshua was trying to show off. It's wild because Joshua was locked in. He was so aligned with what God was doing that he wasn't asking for comfort; he was asking for completion. He didn't pray, "Lord, help me survive this!" He prayed, "Lord, give me the time to finish what You told me to do!" That's a different kind of man right there.

Many of us pray as if we are trying to make it to the end of the day without falling apart:

"God help me stay calm,"

"God help me not lose it,"

"God help me get through!"

These are honest prayers, and God hears them, but there comes a moment when a man needs to pray beyond survival and into assignment.

Some battles will not be won by playing it safe; some chains will not break by whispering polite prayers. Some strongholds will not move until you pray like you believe God is still God. Joshua requested more time because he knew the mission mattered and trusted the God who called him to it.

Here is what I want you to see. Bold prayer is not reckless emotion. Bold prayer is faith with its shoulders squared. It is a man standing in the middle of pressure, saying, "God, I believe You can do what I cannot do, and I am asking You to move in a way that only You get credit for."

So, let's get practical. What have you been tolerating by praying *around* it rather than praying *through* it? What have you been managing because you stopped believing God could actually change it? If God is calling you to freedom, purity, healing, leadership, or restoration, then it is time to pray as if that is possible. Not because *you* are powerful, but because *He* is.

Today's Battle Plan

"Now to him who is able to do immeasurably more than all we ask or imagine, according to his power that is at work within us, to him be glory in the church and in Christ Jesus throughout all generations, for ever and ever! Amen."
— Ephesians 3:20–21, NIV

God is not intimidated by the size of your request. When your prayer lines up with His purpose, you can ask big and still stay humble.

Take the Next Step

Pray one bold, God-sized prayer today, out loud, not in your head. Write it down, then take one aligned action that proves you meant it, a call you need to make, a boundary you need to set, a step of obedience you have been delaying.

The Truth You Need To Face

1. Where have safe prayers replaced bold ones in your life?

   ____

   ____

   ____

2. What do you sense God challenging you to believe Him for right now?

   ____

   ____

   ____

3. What is the real reason you hesitate to ask God for the impossible?

   ____

   ____

   ____

DAY 19:
Don't Let Them Up

You weren't saved to survive; you were called to conquer.

"When they had brought these kings to Joshua, he summoned all the men of Israel and said to the army commanders who had come with him, 'Come here and put your feet on the necks of these kings.' So they came forward and placed their feet on their necks. Joshua said to them, 'Do not be afraid, do not be discouraged. Be strong and courageous. This is what the Lord will do to all the enemies you are going to fight.'"
— Joshua 10:24–25, NIV

Inside the Fight

Joshua is not being extra. Here, Joshua is being intentional. God gave them victory, but Joshua knew that victory had to be owned, not just observed. So he called the commanders forward and made them put their feet on the necks of those kings. That was not about humiliation. That was about authority. He was teaching them what it looks like to stand over what used to intimidate you. He was putting a lesson in their body, not just in their head, so they would never forget who God made them to be in the fight.

Here is where it gets real for men. A lot of us have settled into management when God is offering mastery. We manage our temper rather than surrender to it. We manage lust instead of killing it. We manage addiction by hiding it better. We manage compromise by calling it progress. And the whole time, God is saying, I did not free you so you could keep negotiating with what used to own you.

Partial obedience always leaves a door cracked. It leaves room for the enemy to come back, not always louder, but smarter. That is why Joshua draws the line. The fight is not over when the enemy is down. The fight is over when the enemy is dealt with, and when you decide you are done cohabitating with what God told you to conquer.

Lean in here. You cannot heal what you keep excusing. You cannot overcome what you keep entertaining. The man you are becoming cannot be built on secret agreements with the very thing that keeps trying to destroy you. God did not save you to make it by the skin of your teeth. He called you to walk in complete freedom, and full freedom requires full surrender.

Today's Battle Plan

*"Submit yourselves, then, to God.
Resist the devil, and he will flee from you."*
— James 4:7, NIV

Resistance is not passive. It is active. When you submit to God and take a stand, the enemy loses ground, and you stop living like a victim of what God already broke.

Take the Next Step

Identify one issue you have been managing instead of conquering. Say out loud, I have authority in Jesus to overcome this. Then take one bold action today that shuts the door, deletes the access, cuts the supply, confesses the secret, sets the boundary, and does it like a man who is done negotiating.

The Truth You Need To Face

1. What issue have you been managing that God has been telling you to put to death?

2. How has partial obedience been robbing you of complete freedom?

____

____

____

3. What does walking in authority look like for you today, and what action will prove it?

____

____

____

DAY 20:
Keep Taking Ground

If you're not dead, you're not done.
"So Joshua took the entire land,
just as the Lord had directed Moses, and he gave it
as an inheritance to Israel according to their tribal
divisions. Then the land had rest from war."
— Joshua 11:23, NIV

Inside the Fight

Joshua did not stop after Jericho. He did not stop after Ai. He did not stop after the five kings. He kept taking ground until every promise God spoke became a living reality for the people he was leading. Here is the part a lot of men miss: a breakthrough is not the finish line; it is proof that you can keep going.

Here is what I want you to see. Many men plateau because they confuse a win with completion. You finally get some momentum, your marriage improves a little, your discipline improves, your mind gets clearer, and you start coasting. You loosen the boundaries. You skip the prayers. You stop doing the things that kept you strong. Not because you mean to drift, but because relief can make a man careless.

Joshua teaches a different kind of manhood. He kept taking ground until the job was done. That does not mean he was frantic. It means he was faithful. He understood that his obedience was not only about him. The ground he took became an inheritance for others. His leadership built a future for families who would come after him. That is what real men do. They do not just win for themselves; they win for those connected to them.

Lean in here. Your growth is not private. Your obedience has an impact. The way you show up matters, because someone is going to live under the shade of the tree you plant. That is why you keep taking ground. Not because you are chasing applause, but because you are carrying an assignment. There is more in you, and there is more ahead of you, and God does not waste the fight; He uses it to build a legacy.

Today's Battle Plan

"Let us not become weary in doing good,
for at the proper time we will reap a harvest
if we do not give up."
— Galatians 6:9, NIV

You are not behind, and you are not finished. The harvest is connected to endurance, so stay faithful and keep moving forward.

Take the Next Step

Name one area where God is still calling you to grow, and write down one next step that proves you are still advancing. Set a time this week to act on it, then follow through even if you do not feel motivated, because momentum comes from movement.

The Truth You Need To Face

1. Where in your life have you been tempted to coast on past victories?

____

____

____

2. How does your obedience today impact the next
   generation, the people watching you, and the people
   connected to you?

   ____

   ____

   ____

3. What new ground is God asking you to take right
   now, and what will your next step be?

   ____

   ____

   ____

DAY 21:
Choose Your Legacy

Legacy is built one choice at a time.
*"But as for me and my household,
we will serve the Lord."*
— Joshua 24:15, NIV

Inside the Fight

Joshua is not giving a hype speech here. He is drawing a line in the sand. After everything they have walked through, after battles and breakthroughs, after victories and failures, he gathers the people and makes it plain. *Choose.*

That is where authentic manhood lives. Not in emotional moments. Not in conference highs. Not in a strong week. Authentic manhood is proven in everyday obedience, when nobody is clapping, and nobody is watching, when life feels ordinary, and the only thing holding you steady is conviction.

Here is what I want you to see: Joshua does not say, "As for me and my household, we will serve the Lord when it is *easy*." He does not say, "We will serve the Lord when the music is playing." He says, "We will serve the Lord. *Period*." That is a man who has decided what he will live for. He has settled his allegiance. He has come to terms with the cost. He is not drifting anymore.

Many men want a legacy, but they do not want the weight of leadership that comes with it. Legacy is not built by what you post. It is built by what you practice. It is not built by intention. It is built by repetition. One choice at a time. One boundary at a time. One prayer at a time. One act of integrity when it would be easier to compromise.

Lean in here. Serving the Lord is not just a private belief; it is a public direction. It shapes how you treat your wife, raise your children, and handle your money. How do you speak when you are angry? How do you respond when you are tempted? It shapes the atmosphere of your home. Joshua understood that, and he refused to let his household drift into divided devotion.

Here we are, at the finish line of the journey. However, this is also the starting line of the rest of your life. These twenty-one days are not meant to be a moment. They are intended to be a marker. A turning point. A decision that you do not just feel, you *live*.

So here is the question: *Who will you be*? Not on your best day–on your typical day. The man you become in ten years will not be the result of one big moment. He will be the result of the choices you keep making when life is quiet.

Today's Battle Plan

"Seek first his kingdom and his righteousness, and all these things will be given to you as well."
— Matthew 6:33, NIV

God does not bless divided hearts. When you put Him first, He puts in order what is out of place and strengthens what is under pressure.

Take the Next Step

Declare it out loud today, "As for me and my house, we will serve the Lord!" Write it somewhere visible, then choose one practical habit that reinforces that declaration: a daily time with God, a weekly check-in with your wife, a boundary with your phone, a commitment to community, and start it today.

The Truth You Need To Face

1. What kind of man do you want to be known as ten years from now?

   ____

   ____

   ____

2. What habits and choices right now are shaping that future, whether you realize it or not?

   ____

   ____

   ____

3. What will it take for you to serve God with consistency, not just intensity, and what will you change starting today?

   ____

   ____

   ____

Conclusion

You made it! If you are reading this, it means you did not just skim ideas; you stepped into the fight. You showed up for twenty-one days, not to collect information, but to let God form something in you, and that matters because most men do not struggle with knowledge; they struggle with follow-through. The fact that you stayed with it says something about the man you are becoming, and I want you to hear this clearly: this is not the finish line; it is a marker.

The battles Joshua faced were real, but they were never only about the land. They were about the man who had to become strong enough to steward what God was giving him, and the same is true for you. The goal was never to read a devotional and feel inspired for a moment; the goal was to build a foundation you can live on when life gets loud again, and pressure tries to pull you back into old patterns.

So here is the question: *What happens next?* Because the enemy loves it when men get stirred up and then do nothing with it. He loves it when a man has a great week, a strong month, a decisive moment, and then slowly drifts back into old habits because nobody else knows, nobody else is walking with him, and nothing changes on the calendar. Do not let that be your story.

Build on what God has done in you by staying consistent. Keep showing up, keep praying, keep fighting the fight, keep taking ground, and keep choosing your legacy one decision at a time. The forging does not stop because you reached the end of these pages; it continues every time you decide to obey when it would be easier to coast.

And do not keep this to yourself. If this book strengthened you, it can reinforce another man. You know someone tired, stuck, drifting, carrying shame, trying to be strong with no support. So, invite him into the fight with you! Start a conversation; text him today, and say, "Let's go through this together, because it does not have to be complicated." Then, give him a copy of this book!

Proverbs 27:17, NIV says, "As iron sharpens iron, so one person sharpens another." If it takes iron to sharpen iron, it takes a man to sharpen a man, which is why you do not have to do this alone. Grab coffee once a week, read the day together, talk through the questions, pray for each other, and hold the line. Why? Because *that* is discipleship; *that* is brotherhood; and *that* is how men are forged and how men change.

Better yet, start a small group and gather two to ten men. Use this book as a resource; not as a way to impress each other, but to be honest, build discipline, heal, grow, and become the kind of men whose families feel safe, whose integrity is real, and whose faith shows up in everyday life. The world does not need more men who can talk about strength; it needs men like you who are becoming strong.

Here is my encouragement as you close this book: do not sit on what God gave you, and do not let it fade or stay private. Be proactive, share it, build with it, and let other men be blessed by the wisdom you gleaned. God can use your growth as a doorway for somebody else's breakthrough. The battle is not over; in many ways, it has just begun. So, live like a man who is *forged in the fight*.

About the Author

Jose Vasquez is the Lead Pastor of Church at the Bridge in Newburgh, New York, a multiethnic and multigenerational church rooted in helping people make a real connection with God and with one another. He is a husband, a father, and a shepherd at heart, passionate about walking with people through the real battles of faith, identity, and purpose.

Jose writes from lived experience, not theory. His heart is to help men grow stronger on the inside, develop spiritual discipline, and learn how to walk with God daily, not just when life is loud or convenient. Whether preaching, mentoring, or writing, his aim is always the same: to help people encounter God in a way that transforms their lives.

To learn more about Jose's ministry and ongoing work, visit josevasquez.online. You can also connect with him on Instagram at @pjosevasquez.